JOSIE SLATON TERRY

Healing Your Thoughts

ISBN: 978-1-947476-00-4

Published by

Alibi Publishing and Entertainment

1415 Hwy. 85N Suite 310-462

Fayetteville, Georgia 30214

alibipubandent@gmail.com

Visit our website at AlibiWorldEntertainment.com

To protect privacy some names in this book have been changed and some of the definitions are based on the author's interpretation. All scripture references are taken from the King James Version Public Domain.

This book is intended as a reference and motivational book only. It is not intended to take the place of medical advice from your physician or in rendering any legal advice.

If the details of your situation are fact dependent you should additionally seek the services of a competent professional.

ACKNOWLEDGEMENTS

First I would love and have to give great honor and all glory to God, the healer. Without you, Lord...none of this would've been possible. Thank you.

My heartfelt thanks goes out also to my husband, Clyde for his years of constant love and support. In your own special way you have stood by my side and allowed me to do what I love most. Thanks.

And to my sister, brothers, and extended overwhelmingly amount of nieces and nephews...*Wow,* where would any of us be without family.

Thank you again, to *Fabulous over Forty Networking* and all of my Social Media related or based friends and associates. Let's keep doing what we do.

My readers...what can I say? I appreciate each and every one of you. Each page turned represents a part of me that can never grow tired or lose interest in showing my gratitude for your belief in me and years of purchases and support.

And now to my friend and publisher, A.e. Santi...thank you for allowing me to use ALIBI as a platform to release this project on a national level and for dedicating your time, efforts, and expertise...and also, for the encouragement to do it again.

A special thank you to the staff of ALIBI...we did it!

God bless you all

Healing

Your

Thoughts

by

Josie Slaton Terry

Edited by A.e.Santi

For

Alibi Publishing and Entertainment

TABLE OF CONTENT:

(Continued)

INTRODUCTION

This book is to help you realize that your negative thoughts do not have to control you and have you living defeated.

Healthy thinking comes not by birth, but by choice.

It is a conscious decision made daily to think healthy thoughts and speak words of life to yourself as you enter these various stages of life:

(a) Birth

(b) School

(c) Marriage

(d) Job/Career

(e) Friends, etc...

The thoughts you think and the words you say will keep you sane...or drive you insane.

Many people are not aware of how their unhealthy thoughts and words, even in teasing, are unfruitful seeds. Sick thoughts will imprison a person's true purpose.

Some people's thoughts have kept them on a welfare roller coaster that has been passed down from generation to generation.

The reason is simple...*no one healed from the negative mindset of poverty.*

The book of Proverbs says...As a man thinketh in his heart, so is he.

Healthy thoughts lead to making better decisions and a happier lifestyle. This book is to open the consciousness of your mind to see that life is more meaningful when your thoughts are well and strong. The richness of life is in the thoughts and the power of the tongue. Get the thoughts right and the tongue will follow.

Healing Your Thoughts is a book written and designed to bring to light how the mind must rid its negative mindset in order to have a healthy and positive lifestyle.

CHAPTER 1

POSITIVE vs. NEGATIVE

Studies reveal that positive thoughts heals the mind, the body, and the soul. Even redirecting a life of destruction to a life of purpose may be achieved through proper techniques and thought patterns.

Another study said how even plants lived longer when cared for with kind words while the plant without the loving words died sooner. Now, while this is being said about the life of a plant imagine how thoughts and words can make or break *your* life.

When you confess the scriptures or positive affirmations, believing the words that you are saying, your body becomes peaceful and hopeful expecting something good to happen. That is why the *Vision Board* practice is so widespread now. Training your thoughts and words to see possibility gives hope in achieving your life's goal. With all the bad news around, good thoughts must be downloaded into your memory bank and repeated often. Which also means having relationships that build you up and not tear you down.

One day while I was with a friend, my friend kept talking about the things that hurt her from many years ago. The recollections to her were as fresh as if they had happened only days earlier. Her conversation contained and revealed many unhealed and painful thoughts.

Trying to get a person to release unhealed thoughts can oftentimes get your own feelings hurt. Unhealed thoughts can stay with a person until their dying days. It is also said that unhealed thoughts hide behind alcohol, addictions, anger, bad behavior and pride.

Many people are not aware of how their unhealthy thoughts and words, even if teasing...are unfruitful to their life as well as others. Sick thoughts will imprison an abundant lifestyle and prohibit the purpose of life.

In other words...what you think, becomes you and/or a part of you.

Consider your thoughts and make the adjustments with thoughts that will keep you healthy and prosperous in mind, body, and soul.

When a thought occurs in your mind, especially when you are about to make a significant decision, you should take a moment to figure out if it is a good thought or a negative thought.

Ask yourself if you are thinking that particular thought based on past judgments or agony.

Do a checklist within yourself to figure if the thoughts are effective or worthless.

Some people allow their thoughts to run rapidly and as the old saying goes, "loose lips sink ships."

Wrong thoughts have destroyed many relationships. Realize that the freedom of thinking is a blessing from God.

How the mind is used, supplied, organized, cared for, handled or mishandled is your free will. If not handled correctly it will sometimes cause the sufferings that you think that may have come from God, to destroy you. Even when others are at fault to what's hurting you...you still have to forgive them to live your best at life.

Wake up with good thoughts, greet your day with good thoughts, and retire with those same good thoughts.

Don't allow anything or anyone to choose or steal your thoughts replacing them with their own. Remember...you are the captain of your ship.

If negative thinking tries to control you, you can stop it. It's within your power. It's up to you to control your mind even though you must fight for that control.

Is it possible to have peace of mind during chaos? If you set your mind to see the rainbow, yes...the storm will soon be over. Negativity can not keep a good man or woman down. Positivity will definitely harvest good thoughts and almost guarantee a persuasive outcome. Victories occur in positive soil even when others are speaking critically against you. It's your words that produce growth in your life, not their words unless you receive them.

With this power comes energy to plan and to create.

Healthy thinking helps you to become a better person. You become the engineer of what you think and say because you are aware of the power of words and thoughts.

Positive thoughts are on the side of love while negative thoughts are most times on the side of hate...and the one you feed will always travel with you. Know that what you attract is based upon what you think.

One day after preparing myself for my *I am ready for the world* mindset someone called me with negative news by sharing something that someone had said about me. Normally I shake off negative news that carries no truth but for some reason this time I dwelled on it.

Though I never questioned as to why it was said I allowed it to eat at me all day long. It wasn't until much later that I realized that I hadn't allowed any good thinking or thoughts to settle into my thinking all day. Instead, I allowed all negative thoughts to be played as if they were on repeat.

Finally I realized that negativity can catch you off guard. But listen, it can't stop the good things from happening for you. When you turn away from the deceitfulness of mind games you'll avoid the crazies and gravitate toward people who *are* somebody.

If you are feeling defeated or overwhelmed change the negative thinking with positive thoughts and positive outcomes will start happening. Become aware of the ill results of negative thinking and stay focused on what you are saying and thinking to yourself. It is so beautiful when your words and thoughts are working for you and not against you.

Think of it like this...a negative thought about or toward yourself, regardless of whether you said it or someone else said it, is a lie. One of my favorite quotes that came from my aunt was, "...a lie doesn't care who said it."

Once you keep saying it to yourself or listening to others negative comments you will eventually begin believing it to be true.

My aunt also said, "...a lie will outlast the truth."

This saying can also be right for a negative thought. It can and will *outlast* the fact if you allow it to.

Remember that.

CHAPTER 2

THE THINKING MIND

Albert Einstein, a great Physicist said, "The world as we have created it is a product of our thinking. It cannot be changed without changing our thinking."

As said earlier, thoughts can be helpful or harmful.

When the mind is clear an awakening takes place at each intersection of life to help you live an abundant life. Understand that at every stage of life your thoughts need healing and a break from the *problems* and *cares* of whatever is happening during or before that time.

When you are caught up being everything to everybody else you become tired and you can lose your positive mindset. That is when it is time to do inventory on *yourself*.

Your prayer should be like Jabez's prayer..."*Lord bless me indeed.*"

This is not a selfish prayer because before you can continue to go out and inspire the world your thoughts must be refreshed. This means taking your name off of everyone else's agenda and taking a *selfish* inventory of your own situation and life. This hits home for me because I was and may well be still the person who *wants everyone to love her.*

However, I am also the person who practice what I preach. I do put in the time to heal my thoughts and make it a life practice. As we live day by day we have to exercise not only the body but also the mind.

When I was a child my mother gave me *Castor Oil* for a good cleansing and as each of us can attest, it was nasty. Very nasty. With that said, the mind needs a good cleansing from the pollution of our past hurts and pains.

All the negative thinking and thoughts that are just sitting there stinking up your life...*they need to go.*

That mind that is so full of congested thoughts...*needs to be flushed out.*

Whatever thoughts that you have that's making you frown ...*those thoughts need to go.*

Words causing a sinking and tightening in your stomach...*must go.*

You can't sleep tossing and turning...*those hidden and subconscious thoughts need to go.*

In the bible Jesus said to cast those worrisome thoughts on him because he cares for you. Just take your time and work on one thought at a time. When it comes up flush it out with a good word or thought.

Another reason to beware of the negative thoughts is because they are not your true way of thinking:

"You will never get it right."

"Nobody likes you."

"You know you are the oddball in the family."

"or...the blacksheep."

"You will not be anything in life."

All lies...lies, I tell you.

Some people not only listen to negative self-talk but try to fit those words into their lives. It's like trying to put a square peg into a round hole. The mind works overtime with the negative thoughts that do not belong to you. Thoughts must be supplied to find ownership. The only power a negative thought has is what you give it by believing the lie or holding on to the hurt that it reminds you of from the past.

Staying focused on a *bigger than life* positive concept can help change what you are thinking. You are your thoughts doorkeeper. Stop allowing in what you don't want in.

If robbers were at your door trying to get in would you freely open the door and welcome them in? No. So why is it that you would open your mind and welcome in the thoughts that are robbing you of your peace and joy?

Someone once said, "...just because the wrong thought came in does not mean it has to stay and build a home."

The thoughts you think are in a battle...negative in opposition of the positive. Negative thoughts will always sabotage peaceful thoughts. It's the good versus the evil.

However, the healthy new way of thinking can win over the old thoughts with willpower. Meaning using self-control.

God has given you this incredible armor to suit up.

Wherefore take unto you the whole armour of God, that ye may be able to withstand in the evil day, and having done all, to stand.

Ephesians 6:13

CHAPTER 3

THERE IS A BATTLE GOING ON

You have grown and changed with life. Yet, you can't see how much you have changed. But now that you are older there shouldn't be any way that you would make those same crazy mistakes that you made when you *were* that younger person. So the question is...why torture yourself *now* behind what happened back then?

This battle of the thoughts that's in your mind can be won. You don't have to have your thoughts continuously tormenting you while at the same time giving you nightmares and health problems.

Negativity thinking is a crazy type mode of thinking over simple matters. To bring about the change in your thoughts you must stay on guard over what comes into your mind and what goes out your mouth.

Trust...it is not a one time thing and it is also easier said than done.

Some steps to take:

1. Accept that negative thoughts came from something that hurt you.

2. Try not to meditate on the thoughts.

3. Over power the negative thinking with positive music and messages.

4. Get professional help if you cannot stop the thoughts from tormenting you.

Getting rid of negative thoughts altogether, especially at once, could more than likely end up in a seriously *til the end* mental fight.

The old thoughts do not want to give up the territory that they have ruled over for years. Even when talking with people who are buried in negative thinking they will actually get mad with you when you try to help them. Negative thinking has a power of ownership. It will not leave willingly.

Some people believe that hurt is passed on. So, whoever takes on the role of being the one to pass on hurt, trust...they somehow at some point were once hurt themselves.

You can be the one to stop the hurt and heal the next generation.

Negative thoughts can be like the game *Monopoly*. They want to control your every move and buy up all your time. So stay free from words that keep you locked-up inside.

Some people cannot express themselves because they let their thoughts convince them that they are shy. Positive thoughts will balance and give you confidence you while negative thoughts can coincidentally keep your life off balance.

But remember...the battles of *your* life were won at Calvary.

You can be more than you are or were with a change of a thought. Is there anything too hard for God? Whatever hurt you have you can be healed once your thoughts agree with the Word of God for healing:

He sent his word, and healed them, and delivered them from their destructions.

Psalms 107: (King James Version)

Day by day we fight to gain more strength from our weak thoughts. To launch into a higher way of thinking means healing the thoughts that supported the wrong belief system that came in through parents, school, or friends. These thoughts have roots in your system. They cannot and will not leave without a fight.

Yet the bible encourages us to fight a good fight of faith.

Righteous thoughts are to us like honey is to the bees; sweet to the soul. They help us to enjoy life. Thoughts speak to your purpose and if you think you can do it, you will do it.

So, if nobody else believes in your dream you can still push yourself to succeed because your thoughts support your will.

When there is a lack of *peace of mind* the bible says that strongholds *(thoughts that should be pulled down and taken captive)* are invading your mind. You must erase and delete a negative thought in order to see the real picture of your purpose. The way you live, see life, and judge others comes from these thoughts. It may sound crazy but talk to yourself and ask questions like:

"Where did that thought come from?"

"Is this thought true?"

"Was that a thought I picked up from someone else's life?"

Worrisome thoughts have no value or purpose.

After questioning the thoughts you will notice that they will stop.

A thankful mind will put negative thoughts out of commission. Strengthen up with prayer and praise. When confronted with thanksgiving, negative thoughts are beaten down.

CHAPTER 4

WHO IS THE BOSS?

You are not locked down to what you think. Meaning, you are not limited without any way out.

You can think outside of the box.

The mind was wired up to be dominant. It can turn a life of rags into a life of riches. Your body has many members...however, the brain is the boss.

Thoughts can be wild and disobedient. Wild and funny. Sad or happy.

Whatever the case, you are the driver.

Look at your thoughts like little children. They need to be brought up to give you respect. When your thoughts feed you defeating mood swings and negativity thinking that is a disrespect to your ability to live life as your best self. Your worth is in your thinking and words.

The other day I heard a woman tell her friend to look for her body to have back problems because everyone of her body-build eventually *will* have back problems. That is an invitation in her mind that is disrespecting to her livelihood.

Even when you experience pain or setbacks your thoughts don't have to print a negative picture of things to come. This way of thinking and accepting things the way they are and expecting less takes away the power to believe in the best that life has to offer to you.

Your thoughts are also as a puppet.

You give them life by pulling the strings.

Thoughts create a successful or unsuccessful life based on how you believe and respond to them.

Your positive thoughts produce results. Whereas the wrong thoughts produce results as well. They both need your approval to supply them with access.

Whichever one is given the passage creates the outcome.

For example:

If you have joyful thoughts the positive thoughts ruled.

If you have low self-esteem thoughts, the negative thoughts ruled.

Abusive behavior is a product of negative thoughts.

The question is, "Which one you are you feeding?"

The right thinking has more power than the wrong thought. It's just that the wrong thoughts have been given more time to grow.

How can anyone come out of a smoke-filled room and not smell like smoke?

If the company you keep and your environments are negative the wrong thoughts have had good ground to grow over the years. The sad story behind this is the unfruitful thoughts bear no seed for a fruitful life.

No matter how you try to win the negative thoughts will always be there to remind you of your mistakes. The only solution to this problem is to do self-help on your mind and be determined to stop the madness.

I know of people who have allowed their controlling and negative thoughts to drive them crazy.

I met a lady who came in to my business as a customer. She was a very *booksmart* lady with many degrees behind her name. Nonetheless, she had some crazy thoughts going in and coming out of her mind of someone following her.

Wow.

She showed me some of the books she had been reading.

They were all dark and fear-based books.

I wanted to share with her my concerns but she was too *smart* for me. She allowed her thoughts to tell her that people were against her. The ending of her story was her family having to place her in a facility to help her come back to reality.

Her thoughts had driven her crazy and unbalanced and caused great pain to her family.

Another lady I met told how her thoughts almost drove her crazy over a man she once loved.

He walked out of her life and moved to a new city.

She knew that he was in this city and was staying at a hotel but she didn't know which hotel. So, she got on the telephone and was calling every hotel in this large city trying to locate him. She had even gotten on a flight and went to the city to find him. Ofcourse it was like a needle in a haystack.

She had no clue how to find him yet she had called hotel after hotel looking for him. As a result of her search she said that she had felt herself going into this deep dark space in her mind and she immediately cried out to God to help her.

That is what brought her back to reality.

Believing in her every thought about wanting a man, *that she later in life did not want*, almost drove her crazy.

Today she is married and has a happy life with the *right* man that she had met after she had stopped suffering over the wrong one.

Crazy thoughts are just a question away from the truth.

The time it takes to listen and think on the negative thoughts could be time used to question their real purpose and origin which is the first step to getting rid of them.

Fearful thoughts produce hate, worry, failure, poverty and ill health.

Faith filled-thoughts produce love, peace, prosperity, success and good health.

According to 2 Timothy 1:7

We have not been given a spirit of fear, but of power, of love and a sound mind.

CHAPTER 5

WHAT IS FEEDING YOUR THOUGHTS?

What you watch on the television, at the movies, on the internet or listen to through music is feeding your thoughts.

Even your conversations with others are feeding your thoughts.

My niece runs from anything that looks scary to her 2 year old little eyes. But what's funny is she's like this...the more she gets used to something like, lets say a puppy, *real or fake*, she'll want to play with it.

It's the same thing when it comes to what you are thinking. Even negative thoughts. You get comfortable with them and add more negative thinking and habits onto the playlist.

Fearful games or entertainment is not a healthy diet for the mind.

Gossip is not a good dessert to indulge.

If you want to reign in life your thoughts must be kept vigorous. You must stay conscious of your thoughts and meditate on what is right and full of life. That is if you want your best.

To keep a positive mindset you have to identify what is blocking your mind.

This also means possibly changing your entertainment habits.

You must turn the channel from so much depressing news and find the good stuff to feed your brain. Don't give negative people, movies, or even videogames the opportunity to rob you of your blessings.

If you are wondering why bad things keep happening in your life check to see what you are regularly feeding your brain.

Your thoughts must be healed because bad and worrisome thoughts work the mind too hard

I knew this young man who was always complaining about having a headache. A headache can be a product of ones thoughts. Even sickness can start first in the thoughts.

People told the young man,"You are way too young to be complaining about headaches."

Everyone else thought that it was his diet. I, myself, saw more than it being just that.

He listened to loud music that was full of cursing and of hateful words that were vexing his soul.

It was his entertainment that was making him sick.

People are oftentimes not attracting what they want, but rather what they think.

Know that secret thoughts are hiding in your mind and they come out saying *steal, cheat, quit, hate and so on.*

These thoughts bring into manifestation losses, imprisonment, and self-hate. Some of these thoughts unbeknown to the thinker are sometimes generational curses as well.

But, you don't have to succumb to them any longer because you are the master of your thoughts.

God has given you the wisdom, discernment and willpower to weed out wrong thoughts and replace them with precise thinking.

The thief cometh not, but for to steal, and to kill, and to destroy: I am come that they might have life and that they might have it more abundantly.

St. John 10:10

The abundant life starts in your thinking because a healthy mindset is fruitful thinking. There are a resurrection and a more prosperous life for the ones who stay awake to the power of thoughts.

CHAPTER 6

BE SLOW TO SPEAK

When you think about your thoughts, on every significant decision be slow to speak and quick to listen to what those thoughts are saying.

When a determination is made it will either bring suffering or bliss. So, you want to take the time to discipline your thoughts and words.

The point is...you have always had the power of choice over your thinking and your words even if something resulted in you fussing and/or cussing.

It was your choice.

Even if someone made you angry. The words out of your mouth were still *your* words.

At one time in life my dad used profanity *so* comfortably that it was like he was quoting the alphabets. They were his defense against his true battle which was low self-esteem.

But one day he said, "I think a person using curse words do not know of any better words to *express* themselves."

I was so impressed with my dad for telling that or sharing that with me.

They were words of value.

He *felt* he could do better...and he did.

I knew that my dad *knew* better because even my siblings and I were not allowed to use profanity...*which were the same words that he was using!*

Another story...

A friend of mine had shown me a new outfit that she had recently bought. She thought that it was beautiful one though I, on the other hand, had thought that it was ugly.

She also asked me of my opinion of it, I guess looking for me to agree with her.

The thought that it being ugly was an actual thought of mine but it would have hurt her feelings had I told her *my* truth.

She liked the outfit and that was all that mattered.

Understand that this was not a matter of life or death so I chose to think and speak favorably neutral regarding this outfit. I based my response on the fact of being kind to my friend's feelings.

Thoughts are in your control.

It wasn't my thought that matter, it was hers at the time.

In any case, we can think and fit the impression to the occasion. When we control what we are thinking correctly we build up inner strength. The inner power gives us the vision to see and respond to what is good and what may be hurtful to others.

Know subject matters before you are speaking.

Unwise talking can generate wounding thoughts.

Not knowing your thoughts you can speak too quickly or unwisely.

Sometimes you give into wrong when your thinking is not minded and thought out.

You will even sometimes say *yes*...when you *actually* want to say no.

The result will be more of wounded and hurt emotions.

You can use a weak moment to be even more empowered to close the door for good the next time.

When you think before you speak you will draw the right people to you and not run them away. Your spoken word has the power to heal or to hurt. It is still in your power to control what is coming out of your mouth. In fact, the more energy that is given to healing your words the more insight you'll have to see what is yours.

Be quiet and listen to words that others use toward and with you. They may be a right fit for you. Listen closely...are they real or full of fake flattery?

The secret of a successful life starts with how you react, think and speak.

Getting these three in inline is *Fruitfulness in Living*.

Selfishness doesn't care about what is being done, thought, or said.

Sadly, a person like that will never enjoy the spring of joy that pours out of a disciplined mind.

In the book of St. Matthew 12:36 it is said...

But I tell you that everyone will have to give account on the day of judgment for every empty word they have spoken.

CHAPTER 7

FEARFUL THOUGHTS

Fear is like an onion, there are always layers and layers to be pulled off.

When I began dealing with my own thoughts I surprisingly found deeply rooted fear.

My thoughts which were returning and taking me back to my past haunted me. They were fearful thoughts that started in my childhood...and the fear that they caused always had me *overthinking* things.

When you are always trying too hard to figure things out it'll always seem too hard to work things out. I firmly believe that prayer will change things.

That is one of the steps I had to take.

Next, I had to change my way of doing things that kept me in bondage to fear.

When you pray your spirit will reveal to you what you are doing that needs to be stopped, changed or removed. Through meditation I now surrender my heart to God to show me and help to get rid of the different layers of fear showing up as I make various accomplishments.

Most fears will not be known until specific junctions of life are reached.

Jordan, one of the wonderful nephews in my life, had a terrible fear of trying new things when he was quite young.

While visiting with me when he was about seven or eight I took him and his cousin, Erus, to the nearby baseball batting cage.

Erus was okay going in the cage to hit the ball, yet Jordan cried.

Jordan did not want to go into the batting cage and even though he loved softball he felt that the baseball was coming at him too fast. Hitting a ball was okay with him as long as it was softly thrown.

To break his fear I got inside the batting cage myself and started hitting the balls. Jordan began seeing that Erus and I were having so much fun that he now wanted to try it again.

He had forgotten about his fear.

He then got into the batting cage and was hitting the balls left and right. Jordan overcame his fear and grew up to enjoy and actually excel in the sport of baseball.

There was a time in my life when fearful thoughts wanted me to justify why it was okay to keep doing and thinking the way that I was.

Though I had dealt with the subject of confidence in my book *Fabulous over Forty* the fear that I was experiencing in my feelings had me thinking for myself in a different way.

Now, I had to break down *why* I felt the way I felt.

Looking at my fear my thoughts compelled me to be afraid of the business endeavors before me.

Joyce Myers, christian teacher and author says, "*Do it afraid.*"

My nephew Jordan had somehow programmed himself into living a life centered around certain fears that were destroying some of the good things that otherwise he would be enjoying.

I gave his fear a black eye that made things change in his life.

When people tell me I look comfortable doing the things that I do, I know it's because I do it even in the midst of fear.

The challenge is to live a full life...and *that* keeps the thoughts of fear from winning.

If fearful thoughts can be exposed and put on the table at the time of thinking them they would not survive. When they are meditated upon and spoken out against they cannot interfere with one's life as much.

Take for instance, most people fear death and they don't have a reason for the fear.

But it's not death that they fear, it's the way they think about death that causes the fear.

Once you put logic into the *whys* and *what's* causing the fearful thoughts such as the unknown, the rejection, the pain, and so forth, the fearful thoughts have no true foundation to stand upon.

When what you fear no longer has the reservation to live in your thought patterns it gets evicted.

Look...you do not go on the street and pick up strangers and take them home with you, right? Well, treat those unwanted fearful thoughts the same way.

You don't have to befriend thoughts that you do not like. When something doesn't make sense we eventually leave it alone. When fearful thoughts are not making sense vacate them.

Every thought influences another thought.

Fearful thoughts reproduce more fearful thoughts because fear is void of love.

The only way to stop the fearful thoughts is to replace them with loving and confident thoughts.

Someone I met in my office was sharing with me all the calamities and sicknesses of life that alters a person's way of living: a stroke, cancer, a car wreck and so forth.

Stopping him in the midst of his conversation I wanted to know why was he relating his thoughts toward all the bad things that could happen to a person.

He said, "I'm just being real."

His being real was filled with fear and sadly so, being real without love opens the doors to fear...and fear looks at the worst in any situation.

I heard of this man who had thought that someone had stolen his wallet while he was at the store shopping because when it was time to pay the cashier his wallet was not in his pants pocket.

The man went to the service desk to report a robbery just as his cell phone rang. It was his wife calling him to let him know that he had left his wallet at home.

The man had heard so much about other people being robbed from the evening news that the thoughts in his mind were thinking the worst.

He, too, was a victim of a robbery in his own thoughts. His fearful thoughts expected the worst and not the best.

A faith filled thought would have led him to call home and ask his wife if he had left his wallet there but his fearful thoughts were acted out and made him look and feel stupid.

Fear thoughts are void of intelligence, but thoughts without fears will open many doors of opportunities.

CHAPTER 8

THOUGHTS AND FEELINGS

Since taking this new road of understanding how thoughts can heal or hurt I am more focused on keeping my thoughts under control.

Personally, I like the way that it feels.

So many good emotions, outlooks, understanding and a peace of mind come from controlling my thoughts.

Looking in the bible and at life I now know that when change takes place the old surroundings and ways of thinking must be left behind.

I have heard of movie stars and other wealthy successful people who talk about not going back to their old neighborhoods because once you make it you become a victim of its crime. There were even stories reported along the way of some movie stars or their family members being killed in their neighborhoods. *They* changed but their neighborhoods were still in the same mindset of fighting and crime.

I firmly believe in giving back with support and doing whatever is needed to help the community. However, I also think that if there is a lot of darkness in the way of people's thinking the only way the community can be helped is not by blending in but by providing resources that can make the change.

Darkness and light do not go together.

When you are successful and you are in an environment where there is darkness in thinking it will create envy and every evil work.

You could be a victim.

A deeper understanding has to take place before you can reach some people.

If they do not want to turn to God to get free of the sin and darkness then you have to pray afar. People must want to change.

With all the churches, motivational speakers and help centers that are around you would think that there would be less violence. People must make the step to change their thinking and then follow.

The bible says that we cannot put new wine into old sheepskin.

We cannot live a productive lifestyle with old thought patterns. Trying to fit in and thinking about the same level with family members or friends who are still doing wrong things to get by and getting the same results makes no sense.

They will not respect you for pretending to still be like them.

Most people want a person who has a strong thought on life to *prove* that what they have works.

Stay true to your change. Someone is watching and will be helped.

You should never overlook a person because of your success. However, a successful minded person must work in the light to keep their thoughts *fresh and watered*.

Growth is a choice you make about your life.

When President Obama was running for President his light inside changed and inspired the thinking and actions of so many young people.

All my young family members *(first-time voters)* were at the pole in the 2008 Presidential election. They were encouraged by President Obama's ways of thinking and his speaking about change.

The words that he spoke of and the way that he was speaking about change affected their way of thinking about life.

Our thoughts spoken out can be contagious, whether good or bad.

The light from President Obama's thoughts was so bright that my nephews, my-self, and many others waited many hours in long lines to vote...and that was despite the weather conditions.

That is the kind of light that can change a neighborhood and generation. .

Every good deed is a producer of our thoughts.

The teaching of Jesus is that you should be like *the light of the world.*

When the environment is dark it will breed unhappy thoughts. You can not only change your mood but the mood of others. Happy thoughts speak happy words, and pleasant words bring into being happy actions.

Your thoughts should be a light directing our life.

You could be uplifting the space where you live. Getting the mind healthy will get the home together. The home coming together will work on the community coming together. The community focuses on the schools and local government for improvement.

The schools and local government go the next levels of government for change and the progress continues until everyone benefits.

This is the gain of clear thinking.

Thoughts are the weapon of power.

I had this friend who cursed constantly. One day I asked her why did she always used curse words to express herself? Her answer was...because that was her way of getting people's attention. But what she didn't see or think was that the cursing was a turn-off not only to me, but to others as well.

Her thoughts justified her actions.

People most time defended their thoughts or actions because of fear.

The reason they keep these fears is because these fears have them in a clutch. Fearful thoughts can make you lose out on meeting the right people and having the right opportunities develop. It also clogs up your thinking channels and you cannot hear the divine instruction that is trying to get you to the place of your blessings.

CHAPTER 9

ARE THOUGHTS WORKING FOR YOU

OR AGAINST YOU?

Writing this book on thoughts challenged my thoughts.

My mind kept saying, "Josie, this is going to be too hard."

Thoughts can have you questioning how you feel about yourself and why you are doing what you do. No matter if what you are doing is bad or good those questioning thoughts will still come. It's just that the bad thought tries to stop you from doing the good deed.

They *will* disqualify you if you believe them.

Thoughts will feed words of discouragement. They have been the reason many talented individuals have put off living their life's purpose. Thoughts talked them out of their purpose.

One day at the office I received a call from one of my regular customers who was asking me questions regarding her business marketing plans.

While talking about her business plans she slipped in some personal things to me about her boyfriend.

"My boyfriend is a big help to my business but I believe that he's seeing someone else," she said.

Then of course I asked, "...why do you think that?"

"Because," she replies, "he just will not ask me to marry him."

After she tells me all of her thoughts on the relationship I could see that her thoughts were keeping the relationship blocked.

Hopefully I was able to help her know that she was allowing her own thoughts to create situations that may or *may not* have been as accurate as she thought. The only truths that she had was what was present and they didn't prove nor show evidence of him cheating on her.

She admitted that she definitely had not seen him with another woman but her thoughts created another woman resulting in her developing jealousy and suspicious.

Thoughts are powerful and can cause us to live in a make-believe world governed by fear.

Amy is someone I have known for years.

She always lives in fear and worry.

As she has gotten older this fear has picked up more speed.

Trying to get Amy to release her fears was like trying to get her to give up one of her children. In fact, fearful thoughts are like possessions. They even become a valuable gem to the owner.

Amy had not only learned how to live with her fears, but she justified them. She made room for them.

Thoughts cannot heal without our acknowledgment and willingness that they need to be healed.

Finally, to Amy's credit, she was able to start the healing process of her mind from a fearful lifestyle *after being left behind on many occasions by family and friends* to a joyful one.

She finally got it.

She now thinks of the thoughts that she is thinking..if they are good or bad.

Amy said it was hard to admit that the thoughts were not real because she was so used to making a false thought appear true.

Becoming free was an effort. But now...she is free.

All thoughts will bring about an outcome. Some will bring about great success while others such as the wrong thoughts will kill and destroy.

As I studied various people along the way I knew from talking with them that their life circumstances developed from their (unaware) thoughts.

A person with fearful thoughts will manifest bondage into their life.

Hateful thoughts will can oftentimes manifest drought.

Unforgiving thoughts manifest sickness.

Dishonest thoughts manifest poverty.

Angry thoughts manifest confusion.

Surprisingly these people even looked like their thoughts.

But there's a positive side to this too.

Pure thoughts manifest progression.

Happy thoughts manifest friends.

Loving thoughts manifest healing.

Peaceful thoughts manifest harmony, and honest thoughts manifest prosperity.

Controlling the thoughts to what you want them to think will change your outcome from bad to right.

CHAPTER 10

HAPPY THOUGHTS HEALS THE MIND

I heard a story about a wealthy man who had become very sick and was told that he didn't have long to live.

But the man was a worrier...and even with this being said still he never was happy for long periods of time.

Most of the people who worked for him did not like him. In fact, he reminded most if not everyone of a *Scrooge*. But somehow, much to no one's understanding, in his despair he decided to do deeds to *help* others.

The man found happiness in giving and he stopped working so selfishly on his possessions. In other words the man changed his thoughts about life and his health improved.

He lived many good years afterwards as a *changed* man.

Happiness is not based on fame or richest. There are lots of famous and wealthy people who are not happy and there are lots of people with meager resources who are curiously very happy.

I read that giving attention to a single thought for a long time helps stimulate the pituitary gland and as a result can provide a sense of well-being.

The right thinking creates happiness.

Sometimes you try to find joy in others so that you, yourself, will be happy...but It doesn't work that way. Happiness must be for you so that even if the other person is not pleased it doesn't affect your well-being.

Your thoughts can continue to focus on joy and happiness when the desires of the heart are right and your thoughts are not for greed or selfishness.

Another story was of a very successful lawyer who had it all...but was lonely.

He was alone because he thought that making plenty of money and becoming a successful lawyer was all he needed to be truly happy.

In the process of his thinking he forgot about family and close friends.

After reaching the top of what he called success he was still voided of happiness. There was no one around to help him celebrate his riches. Sure, there will always be the material people around who will be there for what you have...but, they'll leave you when your wealth or success is gone.

What he realized was from inside, and that was...he had to become happy and give *out* happiness before he could receive it from others.

You become what you think.

Think happiness, be happy.

Think sadness, be sad.

Worry, despair, and anger can quickly come out of a person with stressful thoughts. These thoughts in some type of weird way can also lead to poor health.

I knew of someone who had a bag of pills and was always trying to get rid of painful and stressful symptoms. The cure to all of their ailments wass in the way that they thought.

If the thinking is right, the action will follow.

There was another person that I knew personally. They died of a broken heart.

This person was engaged to be married but when the other person that they were engaged to left and married someone else...this caused them much shame and disgrace.

The broken-hearted one's thoughts had fed their negative outcome both day and night until the stressful thoughts created health problems and the health problems became the demise to such a promising life when a better gift to the mind would have been to fill it with hope and wisdom for better days.

Understanding your thoughts supplies knowledge for self-control.

Staying in self-control keeps happiness alive.

Keeping an open mind to the possibilities of life will help to improve the state of mind and keep the thinking on track.

I like listening to people who motivate my spirit. Their encouragements keeps my soul fulfilled. Also, I now give my ear to thoughts I want to think on repeatedly and that will always keep me uplifted. But stay away from fearful and hateful words, they are like feeding your thoughts junk food.

The thoughts will tell you, "If you mess up too bad, kill yourself."

With no proof or substance a bad thought will come up first when you are not conscious.

The thinker must stop the thought so that the bad thought will be denied any passage.

It's like being in a Biology class working on a project...these thoughts must be dissected...*totally* from the mind.

CHAPTER 11

DON'T LET THOUGHTS TRAP YOU

You have heard of a person singing off key...right?

Remember how you thought it sounded?

Your thoughts can trap you by having you to *think* off key. But you are ready for a change...and you're ready now!

It could be that the job where you are working is getting on your last nerve.

You want to quit but the only problem is you do not have the proper finances or income to replace it...and your bills are singing, "You owe, you owe!!!" While your thoughts are singing in the back of your mind, "Don't be happy with this horrible job!"

Now to you... the only way you can be happy is if you left that job.

You think that it's your manager, the co-workers, or the customers adding icing to the dilemma...but it's *your* thoughts. Your thoughts are crucial when it comes to making you feel trapped and unhappy.

To get in tune you must capture your thoughts and control your thoughts making them speak to you, not control you. Don't let your thoughts tell you when and where you are to be happy. Being happy is your choice. You must command your thoughts to think of good things...then watch your blessings unfold.

The door to a new job can and will be opened and you can appreciate it more, *if* you stop letting your thought rob you of your peace.

There will be problems on the new job. It comes with the territory, but how you see the problem will be based on seeing the glass half full or half empty.

It will also be based on how you allow your *thinking* to see it.

I heard this story of this man along with his family whose job had relocated him to a new town.

They stopped at a service station and asked the attendant, "What are the people in this town like?"

The attendant asks, "How were the people in the town you just left?"

The man said, "They were the worst people to live around."

The attendant replied, "Well, you are not going to be here long because the people here are about the same."

The man drove off disappointed.

Then another new family drove up obviously arriving through and due to the same scenario.

They stopped at the same service station and asked the attendant, "What are the people in this town like?"

The attendant asked, "How were the people in the town you just left?"

The man said, "They were the best people in the world to live around."

"In fact," the man continued, "it was hard leaving our old town."

The attendant replied, "Well you are going to love it here because the people here are about the same as the people you left."

The man and his family drove off truly satisfied.

It's how you *think* about it and it's your way of being that can oftentimes set the actions of others.

Even being uncomfortable on the job is something to praise.

The discomfort keeps you aware that you should want and deserve more.

Don't curse the thought just control how the thought makes you feel. You will receive more when the time is right...if you believe it.

I once worked on a job that I felt was not treating me fair.

The manager was rude, and I (plus others) was continually bumping heads with him.

I camped out in front of HR every morning trying to see if any other department (within the company) had an opening.

My thoughts were giving me stressful headaches and there was no way I was going to be happy in that department...not working under that *mean* manager. But needing the job I suffered going into work every day.

Then it happened.

I awoke to my real problem...*my thoughts.*

I was in the ladies' room during my lunch-break crying, as I would generally do, out of frustration. This time a different thought came to me.

"What would happen if I approached the job and my boss with love and respect?"

At first I tried to refuse the thought but it began making some sense. I knew it had to be God because the devil wouldn't have me thinking that way nor in the manner of loving someone whom very actions were so rude to me.

My parents taught my siblings and I the power of love and how love will fight your battles.

So, I listened to what this new strange thought was instructing me to do.

While pondering over the original thoughts I wanted to apply them and see where they would lead me. After all, I wasn't getting any place with my old thoughts and I was definitely tired of the headaches.

My attitude changed with forced efforts and I finally got my *love* walk together.

Now look at how the Devil works.

My co-workers started calling me weak.

They saw my change in my duties and to the manager.

Many laughed at me because of my love walk.

I worked with a new attitude.

My thoughts were on the *positive* side of the job and the people in my office.

Within two months a manager from another department came to me and said, "I have been noticing your work performance and I want to offer you a position in *my* department."

The new job position came when my thoughts had changed.

That was the beginning of understanding the power of changing my thoughts and not letting them keep me trapped.

While talking with a woman in her 50's... I will call her Ann.

She was telling me how changing her thoughts saved her marriage.

Ann stopped thinking and speaking discouragement over her marriage.

Her focal point was no longer what her husband *did* or *didn't* do, but now on thoughts that were trying to bring her peace instead.

"Positive thoughts are contagious," Ann said.

When she changed her thoughts her husband could see the incredible woman he had married.

They both wanted to make the marriage work and realized that they had to remove the thoughts that trapped them.

CHAPTER 12

THOUGHTS CAN BECOME A BATTLE

Don't let negative thoughts continuously battle with you.

"You are too old."

"You are too short or too tall."

"You are not pretty enough."

"You can't do it."

They want us to think that we came from the wrong family.

There is a story in the Bible about these two, David and Goliath.

Goliath thought that David was too young and too weak to defeat him. But David thoughts were not fear based.

He responded, "who is this uncircumcised Philistine that he should defy the armies of God?"

David's thoughts led him to *volunteer* to fight Goliath...and he won.

You must go into the fight and into the battle with winning thoughts.

Your thoughts *must* be challenged which can also be accomplished by listening to or reading positive words that overtake wrong thoughts.

I always tell myself that the person I am is the person I was meant to be.

Knowing that God is with me and for me is a thought tool that I use to get me out of the negative thought arena. A person's thought will make or break them because thoughts will shape or reshape the outcome.

In my book *Fabulous over Forty* I was telling how my thoughts battled me for a right turn that I made at a traffic light.

There was a light that flashed and I just *knew* that it had flashed me for a ticket. My thoughts had me worrying about me eventually receiving a traffic ticket in the mail. But it never happened...it was all in my mind.

The thoughts that are at constant battle in our minds can lead us away from the plan of God.

Allow me now to make mention of this lady who was very successful in her business. She also had a very uncontrollable daughter whom she thought would never amount to anything.

As her business, home and husband *(number three)* began failing she lost her hope for life.

Her thoughts led her to suicide. Thoughts that prevented her from seeing that life would get better.

Her thoughts trapped her into thinking that everything that she had done, achieved, or acquired was terrible...especially her daughter.

If she had looked past her dark negative thoughts she would have more than likely seen that her lousy, supposedly no-good daughter had a gift for writing songs. The daughter's gift led her to become very wealthy in just a few years after her mother's death.

Wow!

Negative thoughts do not line up with God's thoughts for us.

The God of the universal thoughts is higher than your thoughts. Releasing your negative thoughts always allow you to see that things will work out for the good.

CHAPTER 13

KEEPING YOUR THOUGHTS FRESH

Word games and reading are ways to keep the mind fresh.

Talking with wise and confident people are ways to keep the mind sharp.

Vacationing where the scenery is stunning will keep the memory fresh.

My sister is a social worker and she noticed the difference in clients' *happy* responses as she resigned them to less television watching and more crossword puzzles and even more outside activities.

The same applies to student and stay-at-home parents. The thought pattern has to have events to keep the thoughts fresh.

My dad had a very sharp mind. Even at seventy-eight his mind was clear and his conversations were meaningful.

He would call me once or twice a week with a good joke. Dad would tell me a joke and I would reciprocate by sharing with him a joke. The moment of laughter for us both was a good mind reboot. I would hang the phone up feeling refreshed in my thoughts.

Dad's method of keeping his mind fresh was through humor.

Seeing the beauty in the day.

Listen to the music that stirs your heart and the beauty that refreshes your mind.

Keep your thought pure.

Your thoughts are available to bring your surrounding into a beautiful place in life. As you do so, cherish the delightful thoughts of others and their ideas.

When you see people who are walking free of fear and worrisome thoughts it is because they labor to be whole in mind, body, and soul. They are not looking for a *lucky star* or depending on the government system to make life work for them.

They get up...and get going.

Fear does not dominate their way of thinking about life.

This is an exercise...

Make two columns on a sheet of paper. In one column list all of your *fearful* thoughts and in the second column list *faith* words to counteract the fear.

Tape it to your mirror.

When fearful thoughts come to mind look at the faith words to erase them.

CHAPTER 14

SECRET THOUGHTS

It is not a secret that *secret* thoughts will eventually make you unhappy. They are dangerous.

Secret thoughts are hidden because they are wrong.

Most times they are full of fantasy, lust, anger, greed, and hatred.

Secret thoughts will also lead you to destruction. They make you feel helpless to change them and they keep your mind working overtime.

Most times you are cautious about your words in public but you say what you want in your secret place. These thoughts are controlling you. You must know that.

You are more than those secret thoughts.

Some people think that a person is not spiritual enough and that that's the reason they have dark secret thoughts. This is not true though it would be wiser not to have secret thoughts lingering in your mind.

People do not start out as rapists, thieves, and murderers. Their secret thoughts are what's dictating the world to them and if they are dark they begin turning into these types of characters because they are relying on *their* inner twisted truths.

Depression is fed from secret thoughts also.

I truly believe that a person thinking or contemplating suicide is listening to dark side of their secret thoughts and these secret thoughts may have started off as harmless, but soon became a barn fire.

Secret thoughts ungoverned can hurt you and so many others. The answer to removing your secret thoughts is to seek freedom from them.

In the book of Ecclesiastes, it says,

that there is a time to be silent and a time to speak.

In my beliefs, secret thoughts should be spoken out to be healed.

God is more than able to deliver you from these secret thoughts. You have to get the ego out of the way and ask for help first though. Once you admit to yourself that these thoughts are not only wrong but that you must let them go, the territory that they once ruled will lose it power. The negative energy they once supplied will be weakened and you will find yourself feeling more alive.

CHAPTER 15

YOU HAVE THE POWER OVER YOUR THOUGHTS

It's crucial to keep in mind that in every situation you have the power over your thoughts.

You have control of stopping a thought whenever you get ready. *You* can make unpleasant thoughts leave.

You can, through effort, terminate a thought and refuse to let it return. Wrong thoughts are in violation of trespassing and you don't have to comply with them.

By having the right to think on happy thoughts, why should you guess on things that you cannot do anything about?

Why even think about other people's problems? Or think on a past that's over? Or believe stressful thoughts of the future that seems impossible to reach right now?

Again, thoughts are controlled by you.

Take back your power from those wrong thoughts and put that power and energy into manifesting the good life. You do not have to believe every thought that you have.

Even when things are going haywire your thoughts can remain calm.

I use the power of *practicing the controlling of my thoughts* in my business.

There was this one incident while working on a job for a client.

The client kept changing the job during the time and it was already being close to a deadline. This was a test, I *think* because of what I already was thinking and wanted to say to this client. But I understood that this was not all there was to my life. My thoughts could observe this confusion but not participate.

The client was trying to cut cost with my time and material. She had lost her calmness and I calmly heard in my spirit, "Take the lead and work wisely to get you both on the right track."

The result was perfect.

She got what she wanted and I got the job finished and was paid. Yet I had to keep a calm head and not just call it quits.

My thoughts were working for me to stay calm.

Bad thoughts will last a lifetime until you put them to death.

People have gone to their graves with crazy thoughts not knowing that thoughts are controllable. When we are awake to what we are thinking we can direct our thoughts towards building up a good day or bad day.

There is this story about someone I know name Melanie. Melanie always had sad thoughts about herself. She never thought of herself as being smart or successful.

One day Melanie came into my office with some of her friends and to my amazement I realized that Melanie's friend had the same thoughts about themselves.

Birds of a feather will flock together.

They were talking down about life and saying life was so hard. It was hard getting through to Melanie because she spent more time allowing her negative thoughts to control her.

Thoughts, you are not aimless.

You are the master of your thoughts and they are to obey you.

The energies of your thoughts should be directed with intelligence and not foolishness. Thoughts need a purpose to think on or have direction.

Think about what you are thinking. The *Law of Attraction* is...a person attracting what they are thinking.

Monitor your thoughts and when an intruder tries to come in sound your conscience alert alarm. You have the power to control your thoughts and determine your destiny.

CHAPTER 16

PLEAD THE FIFTH AGAINST YOUR THOUGHTS

The expression *"I take or plead the Fifth"* coming from the Fifth Amendment to the Bill of Rights is often used in non-legal contexts to convey an unwillingness to answer a potentially embarrassing or incriminating question.

To "plead the Fifth" was a refusal to answer a question because the response could form self-incriminating evidence.

You have the rights to remain silent when being questioned by unwanted thoughts.

The thoughts that are trying to destroy your character, deny them. The thoughts may be right but they are not factual. Remember, they do not have the right to rule your mind.

Refuse the temptation to be tormented by past thoughts that repeatedly remind you of your mistakes and failures. Also, don't think that because the case was tried and you won that you can just move on.

Uncle Joe and your cousin, Joann will remind you of what you did.

The old negative thoughts will try to come back bringing shame.

Once you are recognizing the truth and see how thoughts are working against your mind, health, and relationships the freedom of fact will keep you free from the torment.

Look at life with all its possibilities and see that you can do anything that you have faith in.

See the beauty in your *new*self and allow that old person to vanish.

You can stay free from the enslaved thoughts.

Start a new life: add new routine.

Enjoy the new beginning of the mornings, exercise, and prayer..and keep a right attitude. Also, eat food that is healthy and do activities that you enjoy.

Thoughts vs. Outcomes

- A person who is always uptight has complaining thoughts and friends.
- A person who is insecure is always thinking inferior thoughts and misses out on many opportunities.
- A person who is self-centered is always thinking thoughts about how to get over on someone.
- A person who is peaceful has untangled and soothing thoughts that inhabit their lifestyle.
- A person who is unselfish has thoughts of helping others and many friends.
- A person with a great personality has successful thoughts and a successful life.

CHAPTER 17

WHAT ARE YOU THINKING?

The bible says, *"If anything is excellent or praiseworthy, think about these things."*

Thinking correctly means thinking about what is positive and correct for your situation.

Just because the odds seem to be against you doesn't mean you will lose. When your trust is in God we are not losers, but winners.

God is unlimited in resources, wisdom and whatever we need.

If our thoughts are on *not* having our needs met the cure to that thought is to visualize the abundance of God.

Taking and thinking about life *One Day At A Time.*

Think about how much love God has for you and how He's willing and ready to give you your portion.

Think correctly about the troublemakers.

Most times when your thoughts crowd your mind with the baggage of others you must find a way to move from being around them.

Since no one has the power to take advantage of you without you participating your thoughts should not become a victim of thinking about *them* and the things that *they* do.

Everyone can change the way they think.

Your thoughts must be chosen wisely because your thoughts will create your circumstances, good or bad.

People must stop repeating their same problems over and over to you. You mustn't allow that.

Most times when people be telling you about other people's problems...you are thinking, "What does that have to do with me?"

But the words are causing you to visualize the situation. Correct or wrong thoughts come from what we are rendering our ears to.

My dad had a green thumb. He knew how to grow the best garden.

As I think about his garden the truth came from within the seed.

Every seed produces what it is.

A seed that was planted to grow tomatoes does not grow peas.

This goes back to thoughts.

A negative thought confessed about your lack will not bring about prosperity.

The Bible says...we reap what we sow.

CHAPTER 18

WHAT DO YOU THINK OF YOU?

You are what you think and people see you as you know yourself.

The mind is like a computer. It can store everything.

But there is a time in my business when I must clear off my hard drive.

The same is true with the mind and the thoughts it thinks.

As I stated earlier, bad memories must be deleted.

Who or whatever hurt you truly need to be erased from your mind.

Work on yourself, do not criticize yourself, and *don't* let others define who you should be.

When you are around negative people you feel a drain on your spirit.

There's a sign in my office that reads, *"Everybody brings joy to this office...some when they enter, others...when they leave."*

Negative people break your positive concentration.

I know people who are constantly quoting the bad news reported on TV and I am always thankful that I don't have to go home with them.

Seeing only the bad news makes things look worse than what they may be.

There is good news reported right along beside the bad news but it is the bad news that gets more, if not, most of the attention. That's because more people will easily believe in the bad news because it takes faith to believe that good things are going to happen.

If abusive thoughts continue to formulate, investigate the thoughts. Trace the root of the thought.

The bible teaches us to *seek* and *we will find.*

If you want freedom from the unstable conditions of your life find out why you think the way you do. It could be a generational thing and there could be possible other family members having the same defected lifestyles resulting from their thoughts as well.

You can end it with you.

Change those thoughts.

There is this story of a mother cooking with a small pot...too small for the roast that she was cooking. She ended up trimming a good portion of the roast to make it fit.

Her teenage daughter watching asked why was she cooking in such a small pot that did not have room enough *for* the roast. The mom told her that *her* mother taught her to cook roast...and that she used the same sized pot. Eventually the mother and the daughter called the grandmother to ask her what was the secret to using a small pot.

The grandma answered, "There was no secret in the pot. I just didn't own a larger one so I used what I had."

Stressful thoughts come from worrying and we've all been taught that worrying will wrinkle the face.

I noticed when talking with people with happy thoughts that they looked younger. Also, people with faith in God had more peaceful thoughts. The thoughts that change people from old to young are the forever carefree thoughts.

Thoughts that do not keep one upset by situations are joyful and brings brightness to the body.

"You cannot plow a field by turning it over in your mind."

-Author Unknown.

Good thoughts about starting a new venture does not happen by accident. You have to fire up the wood.

To be a person of destiny the thoughts and plans must be carried over into tangible action because a thought is just a thought. It will go away after a period. If you don't write down a good thought it will be hard to recall it when needed.

Opportunities are always knocking.

If we get up and look for the good opportunities they will be there waiting for us. Each day is a new day for new purposes to fulfill.

Impacting your early waking with prayer and thanksgiving is putting your best foot forward. Remember, your thoughts are working for you or against you. Even though it may look bad it will work for the good if you think it.

Just because you cannot see the thoughts does not mean they are not there and can't take root.

...at work

What you think about yourself will be what others see at the job.

Your workplace, co-workers, and managers are treating you based on how you are thinking about yourself.

No one can treat you bad unless you think it was bad. A bad situation to a person with healthy thoughts is not a curse, but an opportunity.

Rethink your thoughts because you bring about a better situation by what you are thinking. You don't have to settle for thoughts that say you are the wrong age, wrong race, height or whatever the case may be. You may think that you are not smart enough but God has a divine plan for your life.

Always think that God has your best interest in mind.

If a door closes don't think that it is over. If one door closes think on a better door or window opening.

Likewise if someone walked out of your life think about the right person walking *into* your life.

The list goes on...if the job lay you off or you were fired think about how you can now expand your education or skills.

There is always another way of thinking about the situation.

What you continually think upon and train your thoughts toward will eventually come to past. Your thoughts can be based on truth or falsehood, faith or fears.

Use your energy to think positive thoughts and remember that the captain of your ship...*is you.*

You control which energy you want in your life.

CHAPTER 19

YOU CANNOT BASE YOUR THOUGHTS

ON FEELINGS

When we are thinking of a person, place or thing we have to stop adding our two cents into it, and also take note that when things are right we don't have to sugar coat it.

Right thinking is the bedrock of a soul.

The best of life starts in the *thinking mind*.

If you can think clearly about the situation you will spare yourselves the hardship of a relationship that was not right from the beginning.

A person I know name Linda was in love with this guy named Ben. She wrecked and sabotaged her own relationship because she was continually trying to make him jealous, somehow thinking that he would love her more and ask her to marry him if she made him believe that he had competition. Her way of thinking cost her to lose out on the excellent relationship with this nice guy. Her thoughts were not right at all.

Writing your thoughts down can help make sense of them before they are carried out.

Another thing...

When you think you want something...give time to it.

When you keep thinking about something for a long period of time, in the same manner there may be some certainty and validity to it.

I was talking with someone about thoughts and they had all the right words for the conversation.

"I believe in positive confessions," they said.

"I read all of the right books on keeping the thinking powerful," others say.

"Practice what you preach," is what my Dad always taught me.

The words must line up with the action.

For example, I cannot speak on non-violence and go rob someone's home or get into a street fight. My speaking about non-violence would have had no root in me.

The same thing as with thoughts...reading and speaking will not mean a thing without the lifestyle.

When you see people who confesses something but you also see that the actions of those same people are not lining up with their words spoken the best way to deal with the situation is to have no comment.

I am like the old saying that says, "Physician, heal yourself."

There will come a time when you cannot allow others to think for you. Yes, it is wise to get the opinions of others but when it comes to some issues the final thought is on you.

Well, you know of people who love to cook large meals...and they stuff you until you have to unbutton your pants.

My mother was one of them.

She loved to cook and fatten everyone up.

My mother was always good at making desserts seemingly calorie free.

"This is so good *and* it is not that sweet," she would say.

But in essence it was loaded with sugar.

Hence...

Another person's intentions, and that's regardless of how good they may be, should never change the thoughts that you have toward your well being. The relationship should not dominate your thinking of right and wrong.

Giving others the control over what you think is giving them your power. Your mind needs freedom from what others are thinking. The only true thought that you can put your money on is your own positive thought.

There is a joke about a deacon at his church which was near death.

He called the preacher that was over the church to come to his house.

He said, "Pastor, I am near death and I have a great amount of riches stored up. I want to give to the church one million dollars. Please pray for me."

The preacher prayed and asked God to spare the man's life.

The sick man soon recovered and was walking around in good health. One Sunday after services the preacher asked the man what had happened to the one million dollars that was promised to the church?

"Well pastor," the deacon replied, "I thought you would understand that I was so sick that I didn't *know* what I was thinking or saying."

Dwell on that...there's a message in that story.

When I was in art school I had this teacher who was a deep thinker. He looked like a Renaissance man...like William Shakespeare actually. He was so deep in his thoughts that he didn't know how *out-of-touch* he was with his appearance.

He knew what he was doing in the classroom...but outside of the school, he didn't have a conversation.

He looked lost in his thought world.

That is how thoughts can become when you only listen to what is in your mind and never check to see if they are off course or...out of date *(regarding the art teacher).*

CHAPTER 20

HAVING THE RIGHT FORM OF THINKING

A feeling will change.

One moment you'll love everything about a relationship while the next moment you'll feel that that person may not be the right one for you.

If you are not feeling well your thinking starts diagnosing your symptoms with the flu or something. Healthy thoughts will see this as an opportunity to get rest, eat right, or find other solutions. But if you are still dealing with unhealthy thoughts your feelings can lead you into manifesting the flu or any other minor sickness into your system.

Feelings and thoughts can work together for the good but you have to know that *feelings* are only *feelings* and should not be the jury of your thoughts.

Everyone has those days when everything goes wrong.

The children acting up, the dog ran away, the car wouldn't start, and everybody seem to be looking to you for answers.

There are times when you just want to run away from it all.

This is the time to open up your thinking to think above the situation by selecting the clothes that makes you feel good, listening to music that makes you feel good and eating a meal that makes you feel good.

This is called tapping into your feelings.

This is not giving into a temporary situation.

You are controlling how you feel by what you are wearing or doing because you are empowering the positive thoughts.

Everything is based on how you feel about it.

And here's another scenario...

Your spouse comes home tired and does not greet you with a hug nor a kiss. You take it personal and allow your *feelings* to try to figure out what's going on.

In order to see a situation more logically over your feelings your thoughts have to be more precise.

Okay now...

So...you're feeling tells you that your spouse doesn't love you.

You follow up your feelings with thoughts that create argumentum words and now the whole evening is ruined because you did not clearly think about what you were feeling.

Feelings based upon a molehill of results can be turned into a mountain.

Studies show that thoughts materialized in our lives and feelings are sensations that the thoughts *have* to produce. With thoughts you know what it is that you are focusing on. With feelings your attention is unfocused and emotionalized. Therefore, the feelings need the thoughts to judge correctly. Thoughts can rightly judge the feeling's motive and not let them get wild. This comes down to thinking on what is real versus feeling something which isn't as real.

When you dress up in your best attire you feel good.

Beautiful and pure thoughts have the same effect on you as the nice attire.

Keeping your thoughts strong and focused makes your day so rewarding. It happens that way when you don't allow others and circumstances to distract the flow. Don't even allow yourself to be your own distraction. The way you think will change the situation. Just because you *feel* trapped don't make you trapped.

Always stay a thought above how it looks, your situation is subject to change.

Nothing remains the same.

The direction and momentum will be smooth sailing for the consistently right thoughts after removing lazy thoughts.

When thoughts are lazy they sink you lower and they manifest negative actions toward the body. But when the body exercises it causes those lazy thoughts to take a hike.

Physical exercise can be beneficial for the mind as well as the body, but it doesn't stop there. They also need to stay in shape by the positive words of the bible and others.

Our body serves our thoughts.

The mind must be used to think of all the wonderful opportunities of life. The more positive words that the mind is surrounded with the stronger the thoughts are. Its purpose is to think clearly and to carry out good judgment in times of trials and tests.

Learning new things like playing the piano or a new dance move is good for the mind.

One couple that I will call Joe and Mary were experiencing family problems with their children...which in turn began leading toward marital problems for them. They had harsh thoughts toward one another and began having frequent disaggrements. One day they received a free gift certificate for free dance classes.

They used the gift certificate because neither one of them wanted to see that certificate wasted.

Learning new dance moves was a good exercise to redirect their thinking. The dance classes changed their thoughts about each other and renewed their thoughts. Their end result was a saved marriage and a different mold of thinking about one another.

Another thing...

Getting involved with healthy activities helps motivate right thinking. The art of learning new things are good exercises for healthy thoughts.

Crossword puzzles and word games are also good mind exercises.

The most excellent exercise for the thoughts is the act of forgiveness and letting go of the past.

People who live in the past are always struggling with problems.

They are overloaded and battling health issues.

Look, we must give our cares to God because they can actually become too overbearing for us.

In the teaching of Jesus we are told to cast all of cares on Him.

My sister, Jean the social worker, visits the nursing home in her city quite often. She always wondered why people experiencing loss of memory could remember the past so vividly. So she feels that people stuck talking about the past don't even know that they are still there.

I know of people whose last accomplishment was ten years ago...and *that* is their conversation.

Recognize weak thoughts and cast those thoughts on God. What can it hurt since you're already thinking that way anyway? The more you clear your mind of defeating and untrue thoughts the more you release the conscience to have confidence in yourself.

But the thoughts need rest.

When Jesus was on the boat asleep during the storm the others were afraid but Jesus spoke to the storm and told it, *"peace be still."*

We can also speak peace into our thoughts.

God has given you the power to direct your thoughts to believe and receive love, peace and happiness...in *this* lifetime.

It is a daily journey but it is a journey that you can win.

The mistake, the past, and the bad reports are changeable.

The strength is in you to not look back or hold on to the weights that say, "you can't do it because it's too hard."

You have untapped power in you and instead of thinking on the problem, seek and think on all the promises of God which say, *"Yes and Amen."*

CHAPTER 21

GET RID OF OLD THOUGHTS

When the mind continues to play over and over old thoughts it's because the former beliefs have made a nest in your memory and they feel at home.

Sometimes it's hard to get guest out of your house when they don't have any place to go they are hoping that they can just hang out at your place just a little while longer. But you know just as well as they do that they've got to go. So...you give them a date.

You must do the same with old negative thoughts reminding you of the gloomy, sad and embarrassing times.

I know this person who cherishes the old thoughts.

Little does he know that the old thoughts are robbing him of a better lifestyle.

When I try to tell him to stop thinking that way, he agrees. Yet the next time I see him he starts again like a broken recorder talking the same old thoughts.

Wow.

How to stop the old thought pattern:

- The first step to healing the old thoughts is to put new thoughts in place of them.
- A daily reading of the Book of Psalms will be an excellent way to wash your mind of old memories.
- If you want to change you have to change the habits that keep you there.

Another thing is to find friends who are uplifting and who want to live a better life. People who think higher and also dream higher...high achievers. Some of your old thoughts could still be on people who you loved, but hurt you. Believe me, you can lose your radiance in pain. But it was a part of the plan.

Isaiah the prophet said, "There is the beauty of ashes, the oil of joy for mourning, and the garment of praise for the spirit of heaviness." You must know that on this journey it is already worked out in your favor. When you change your thinking you change your life. The day will come when the power of wrong thoughts will have no power over you. Use every situation as a part of your journey. When your old thoughts stop operating...life will be better.

CHAPTER 22:

AFFIRMATIONS TO HEAL THE THOUGHTS

Today, I will think on this day with hope.

Today, I will not allow my old thoughts to control my thinking.

Today, I know that I can be happy no matter what comes my way.

Today, I know that I am a winner and not a loser.

Today, I know my best is yet to come.

Today, I know I can be happy.

Today, I will tell the people who matter, *"I appreciate you."*

Today, I will smile more.

Today, I will bless the Lord.

Today, I will take better care of myself.

Today, I will look for the good in me and others.

Today, I will think on this day in the present moment because all is well ahead.

Today, I choose to see this day and everyday as a blessing.

Today, I know that God will not withhold any good gifts from me.

Today, I will walk in love and think kindness with everyone I meet.

Today, I know that the promises of healing, prosperity, and peace of mind reigns in me.

Today, **I walk in favor of God.**

THE END

PUBLISHER'S NOTE:

It is indeed a pleasure to have had the opportunity and the responsibility of not only overseeing this project but to have earned the honor of Branding it and releasing it to the masses as well.

Working with Josie Slaton Terry has given us here at ALIBI a much deserved and appreciated first hand experience at earning an Author's trust along with their unwavering loyalty and respect as we diligently pushed toward perfection while relentlessly giving them our all in professionalism, guidance, and integrity.

We readily offer and extend our services and representation to any other authors who can match up through class, talent, and vision that Mrs.Terry has brought to our company.

In closing...we as a team, family, and force say to all:

Never take for granted your dreams nor your talent as naught.

For from within yourself...grows success

#BBBA

www.ingramcontent.com/pod-product-compliance
Lightning Source LLC
Chambersburg PA
CBHW071623040426
42452CB00009B/1454